PARALLEL REALITIES

PRAJEETA PAL

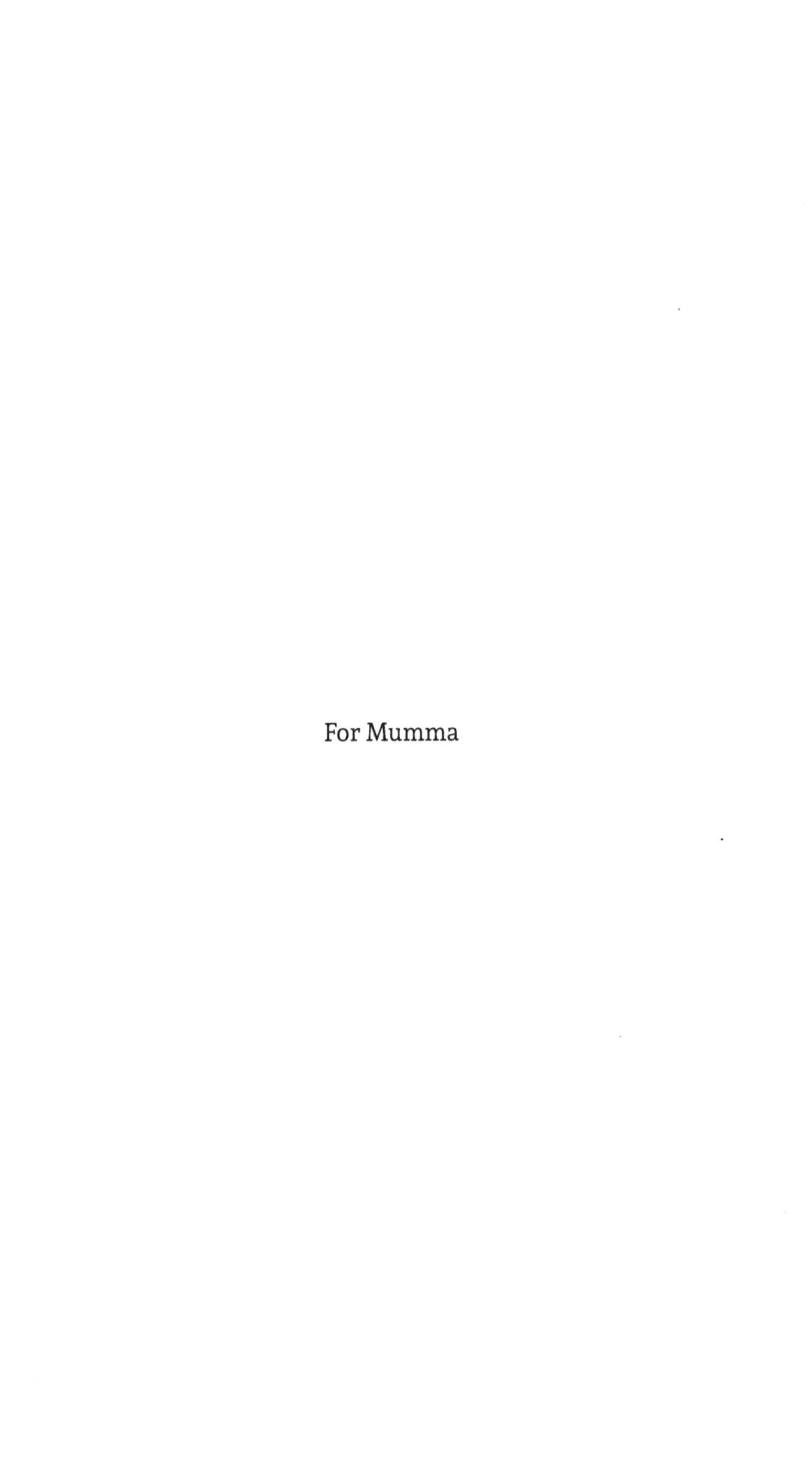

For Mumma

Contents

Foreword

Stories have a way of capturing emotions we struggle to put into words. They let us step into another's shoes, and feel their joys, heartbreaks, and quiet moments of realization. This collection is a journey through those moments—intimate conversations, fleeting encounters, and the delicate threads that connect us all.

Each story here was written hoping that you'll see a piece of yourself in its pages. Maybe you'll recognize the unspoken fears of a daughter, the quiet strength of a mother, and the hesitation of someone standing at a crossroads. Or maybe you'll simply find comfort in knowing that even in life's uncertainties, we are never truly alone.

These stories are not just about endings or beginnings—they're about the spaces in between, where real life happens. I hope you find something here that lingers with you, long after the last page is turned.

-Prajeeta

PREFACE

This collection began as scattered thoughts—fragments of conversations, fleeting emotions, and quiet observations of the world around me. Some of these stories were born from personal experiences, others from imagination, but all of them carry a piece of something real.

Writing these stories was a way of exploring the complexities of human relationships—the things we say, the things we leave unsaid, and the emotions that exist in between. Each character, each moment, is a reflection of the struggles, hopes, and dreams that shape us.

I never set out to tell just one kind of story. Instead, this collection holds a little bit of everything—love and loss, doubt and fortitude, longing and acceptance. I hope that as you read, you'll find something that resonates with you, something that makes you pause, reflect, or simply feel understood.

Thank you for stepping into these stories with me.

Acknowledgements

First and foremost, to my parents, who have been my greatest support in everything I do. Your unwavering belief in me, your patience, and your unconditional love have given me the strength to keep going. Thank you for always standing by me, for never questioning my choices, and for reminding me that I am capable of more than I know. This book, like everything I do, is possible because of you.

To Sagnik Chakraborty, for pushing me beyond my limits and pulling me out of my shell—you saw the stories in me before I did. Your encouragement has shaped not just this book, but the writer I am becoming.

To Sharanjit Pakrasi, for believing in me unwaveringly, even when I doubted myself. Your faith has been a light on the hardest days, reminding me why I write.

To Ayush Basu, for supporting me in every way possible and always finding ways to make me believe in myself. Your presence has been a constant reassurance, and I'm beyond grateful.

To Aieyndree Jha, for listening, for tolerating my endless ramblings, and for always being there with patience and kindness. Your presence has been both an anchor and a safe space.

This book exists because of all of you. Thank you for being part of this journey.

PROLOGUE

Stories don't always begin where we expect them to. Some start in the middle of a conversation, in the pause between words, or in the silence after someone leaves. Others begin long before we realize, stitched into memories, regrets, and the quiet hopes we carry.

This collection is made up of those moments—of connections made and lost, of choices that shape us, of the delicate and messy emotions that make us human. Each story is its own, yet together, they form a tapestry of love, longing, tenacity, and discovery.

Before you turn the page, take a breath. Let yourself step into these lives, feel their joys and sorrows, and maybe, just maybe, find echoes of your own story within them.

Because every ending is just the start of something else.

I

Alternate Universe

Fifteen years since we last spoke. Twenty since I last saw you. Twenty-five since I first met you.

I still remember how you take your coffee, how your favorite meals change with the seasons, the books that draw you in, and the characters you analyze like they're real people. I know the kind of shows you'd enjoy, the characters you'd relate to, and the songs you'd have on repeat—even if they wouldn't be my first choice. I can anticipate your mood after every match your favorite team plays, almost as if it were my own. But for all the things I've memorized about you, the one thing I never could predict was how you felt about me.

Still, whenever I check the score for your favourite team - Manchester United, I wonder what you're doing, because I know you wouldn't miss the game. When I watch the sunset, I wonder if you're watching it too. Some habits don't die, do they?

In an alternate universe, I wouldn't have to wonder. I would know.

I remember your goals, your dreams—the way you spoke about them like they were the only things that mattered. I always knew I wouldn't be a part of that future, and I made peace with it long ago. It never hurt. If anything, I only ever hoped you'd get everything you wished for and quietly prayed for you from afar.

I moved on, and built a life separate from the one where you existed.

Since the last time I saw you, I've met countless people—each unique, yet none quite like you. I've lived through moments you were never a part of, and maybe, at times, I wished you were. Time has moved on. I've changed. And I can only assume you have too.

One afternoon, our paths cross again.

You're back in town—probably for work, probably not for long.

I meet up with some friends, and somehow, you're just there. Seeing you again feels surreal—both familiar and distant. I'm happy, but there's a quiet discomfort settling in my chest. I've never been good in group settings, least of all when facing someone from my past. Last of all you. But you know that, don't you? Maybe you do.

Your gaze lingers for a second longer than it should before you smile.

"How have you been?" you ask.

I force a smile and let out a small breath of laughter. "I'm good. What about you?"

There's so much more I want to say. So many questions I want to ask. But I don't. Because I know you won't answer. Or maybe this time, you will. But I'm too afraid to ask, because the silence that follows would be unbearable.

We laugh, we smile, we talk. And then you ask me to dinner. Just us two.

I don't know why. And I don't know why I say yes. But I do.

My mind is at war with itself—one part urging, 'Just go, have fun, enjoy this moment after so long.' The other whispered, 'Make an excuse, leave before it gets too complicated.'

But before I can decide, we're already in a cab. The city lights blur past, casting a strange glow over this night that feels unreal. We reach the restaurant. It's too late to back out now.

We sit across from each other, only the table between us. A physical space so small, yet somehow, you feel as distant as ever. The restaurant hums with life—clinking glasses, soft murmurs of conversation, the occasional burst of laughter—but it all fades into background noise.

"It's been a long time," you say, running your fingers along the edge of your glass.

"A lifetime," I reply.

You chuckle, a sound that used to be comforting but now feels foreign. "You still analyze everything too much?"

"Do you still avoid answering questions?" I counter.

Your smirk falters for a moment before you shake your head. "Touché."

We talk about everything except what we should. Maybe that's a good thing. Maybe that's how it's meant to be. You tell me about your work. I tell you about mine. You complain about your clients being impossible. I complain about my boss being bossy. You talk about all the places you've traveled. I talk about all the places I wish I had gone.

But there's an unspoken story between us, lingering in the spaces between words. A lifetime has passed, yet in this moment, it feels like no time has passed at all.

And maybe that's what scares me the most.

Am I the one who should talk about it? Should I wait for you to bring it up? Should I just let it go and accept this distance and this strangeness?

You open the door of the restaurant and wave for me to come out. I hesitate, then nod, forcing a smile before walking toward you. Maybe I should just accept this strangeness.

We are in the cab again, and it's awfully quiet. I stare out the window, watching the neon signs flicker outside, illuminating the streets I once knew so well. Our old school comes into view, and I catch a glimpse of the school ground. I almost smile—that's where I first saw you. A lifetime ago. I look away and try to talk to you, anything to break the silence, but then the cab radio plays a song. Forever by Lewis Capaldi.

"Darling, nobody said that it would last forever,

That doesn't mean we didn't try to get there…

I never said that we would die together…

That doesn't mean it was a lie, remember…"

And I stop. No wonder you made me listen to that song—it was a warning, sort of.

"Hey," you call out softly.

I turn to you, but my expression is blank. I don't know what lies behind your eyes or what carefully chosen words you will use to tell me something devastating.

You hesitate for a second, then take a breath. "I like someone," you say.

I exhale slowly. "I know." I always know.

"Won't you ask me who?"

"Not really. I'm sure she's wonderful and most definitely smart because you chose her."

The rest of the ride is silent. The streetlights cast fleeting shadows across your face, but I don't dare look at you. I blink away the sting in my eyes, willing myself to stay composed. As we step out of the cab, I make sure my voice isn't shaky before I say, "So, that was a good dinner. Glad to catch up. See you soon. Bye."

I turn quickly, eager to escape, but you grab my hand. I look up at you.

"It's you, dumbass. It was always you."

"No. It can't be."

"Yes, it is," you insist. "I'm sorry. I was just trying to figure things out, and I know I should have told you. I should have been there. I should have talked to you."

"Yeah, maybe you should have."

Your grip tightens just slightly. "Is it too late now?"

The night air feels heavy like it's holding its breath for my answer. My heart races, but before I can say anything—

My alarm goes off. I wake up. Just a dream.

The sunlight filters through the curtains, casting soft patterns on my ceiling. I exhale slowly, grounding myself in the quiet of the morning. The dream lingers in my mind, familiar yet distant, but I push it away. I have things to do. Another day to live.

I get out of bed, stretching as I make my way to the bathroom. The routine is automatic—shower, coffee, picking out an outfit for work. I settle on something simple, and professional. It's just another workday, and I don't have much to do today anyway. By noon, I've cleared my inbox and wrapped up the minor tasks I had. With nothing urgent left, I take a half-day and head out to meet some friends.

And then, as if the universe wants to mock me, I see you.

You're here probably for work, I don't know, and I don't ask. The meeting isn't planned, but it also isn't unexpected. Mutual friends. A small city. It was bound to happen sooner or later.

I keep my expression neutral, my tone polite. You do the same. There's a carefulness to the way you talk, as if you're measuring your words before you say them.

"How have you been?" you ask.

"I'm good. And you?" My voice is even, professional almost, as if this is just another casual conversation at work.

You nod, offering a polite smile. "Good. Busy, as always."

There's a pause. It's not uncomfortable, just there, like an unspoken agreement to keep things light. We talk about work, about life, about people we both know. There's an ease to it, but also a distance. I notice it, but I don't let it bother me. This is what it is now.

Then, out of nowhere, you say, "Let's go grab a drink. Just us. To catch up."

I hesitate for only a second before agreeing.

We find a bar nearby—quiet, dimly lit, the kind of place meant for conversations rather than loud music. We sit across from each other, the polished wood of the table between us. The bartender brings our drinks, and for a moment, we just sit there, absorbing the moment.

"You always did have a habit of showing up when I least expect it," you say, tracing the condensation on your glass with your fingertip.

"And you always did have a habit of catching me off guard," I reply.

You let out a breath of laughter, something between amusement and nostalgia. "You still think too much?"

"And you still prefer to sidestep things?" I counter, tilting my head slightly.

Your expression flickers—just for a moment—before you give a small shake of your head. "Some habits die hard."

The conversation moves easily, like slipping into an old rhythm we both remember but no longer depend on. You talk about your work. I talk about mine. You mention the cities you've been to. I talk about how I haven't travelled as much as I thought I would. We laugh about how little some things have changed and how much others have.

There's an underlying story between us, but neither of us brings it up. And that's okay. I don't need to ask the questions I once wanted answers to. I don't need to bridge the distance between us. Because I've learned to accept it.

We are two people with a history, sitting in a bar, catching up. And that's all it needs to be.

You push the restaurant door open and wave me over. I hesitate for a moment before nodding, forcing a smile as I step forward. I pause, my feet feeling heavier than they should. Maybe, it's easier to just go along with this unfamiliarity.

We are in the cab again, and you're on a call—animated, effortlessly composed, just like always. I turn to the window, watching the neon signs flicker outside, casting a familiar glow on streets I once knew so well. As we pass our old school, my eyes linger on the school ground. There's no rush of emotion, no wave of nostalgia—just a quiet familiarity, like flipping through an old book whose pages you know by heart. That's where I first saw you. That's where it all began. And that's all it is now—just a place, just a memory.

The radio hums softly in the background. A song plays—"Someone You Loved" by Lewis Capaldi.
"Now the day bleeds into nightfall
And you're not here to get me through it all
I let my guard down and then you pulled the rug
I was getting kinda used to being someone you loved."

As the lyrics play, I realize how much my experiences have shaped me, how much of the past I have accepted without even realizing it. It's not a warning. It's not a message. It's just a song — one that once might have hurt, and now only shows me how much I've moved on, how little power the past holds over me now.

"Hey," you call out softly.

I turn to you, but my expression is calm. I don't know what you're thinking or what's shifted in your demeanor. Whatever it is, I know it's not an apology, not a confession—just something you feel you need to say. You hesitate for a second, then take a breath. "I'm getting married," you say.

I exhale slowly. "Oh."

You nod, eyes searching mine. "I wanted to tell you myself. And... I wanted to invite you."

I let the words settle, let them press against my ribs. "That's nice of you."

You look almost apologetic, but I keep my expression unreadable. "I'd love for you to be there."

I smile, polite and distant. "I'm sure it'll be beautiful."

The rest of the ride is silent. The streetlights cast fleeting shadows across your face, but I don't dare look at you. As we step out of the cab, I make sure my voice isn't shaky before I say, "Well, congratulations. Wishing you both happiness."

I turn quickly, eager to escape, but you call after me.

"Are you really okay with this?"

The night air feels crisp, and indifferent. My heart doesn't race this time. I don't have an answer, and maybe I don't need one.

Before I can say anything—

My alarm goes off, again. I wake up. Just a dream, another dream.

This time, I hope I'm not dreaming. I get out of bed and start getting ready for work—again. After two dreams, you'd think I'd have my outfit figured out by now instead of fidgeting through my wardrobe.

I get to work, slipping into the familiar routine. Later, my friends call, asking me to join them for lunch. I agree, since I'm nearly done with my tasks anyway.

And then, as if the universe had a personal vendetta against me—I see you.

Well, that was unexpected.

We talk like old friends do after years apart—casual greetings, the mandatory "hi's" and "how have you been's?" The conversation flows easily among all of us, light and unassuming. Just as I'm about to head back to work, you turn to me.

"Would you like to have dinner with me?"

I blink. "So, Sam and Zee are coming too, right? Then sure, I'm in."

"No, not really. Just us. Is that okay?"

I hesitate. For a moment, I consider overthinking it—but I don't. Instead, I nod and say, "Umm, yeah, sure. Why not?"

As I step into the cab, ready to finish up my workday, you call out, "I'll pick you up at 7 from your office!"

I glance back, offering a small smile before driving off.

I don't know why you asked me to dinner. I don't know if you'll actually show up at 7. I don't even know if this is real or if I'm still trapped in some dream.

All I know is who you were fifteen years ago. I have no idea who you are now. And I—I'm different too. Life has shaped me in ways I never saw coming, and I'm sure it's done the same to you. So now I wonder—do our changed selves still fit together? Did we ever fit together? Or do we fit better now?

Maybe this is still all a dream in an alternate universe, and maybe this one will have a different ending — but maybe our real ending will remain unfinished.

II

One Cup of Coffee

The city stretched below under the harsh midday sun, the heat shimmering off rooftops and glass windows. He stood at the edge, the glare of the sun stinging his eyes, but he didn't care. One step. That's all it would take. One step, and it would all be over.

What was left to live for? His girlfriend? Gone. His job? Gone. His parents? They wouldn't even look at him anymore, ashamed of what he had become. His friends? They had moved on without him. If he disappeared today, who would even notice?

He inhaled sharply, closing his eyes as he braced himself for the fall—

"Hey! Stop! What the hell are you doing? Are you insane?"

A voice cut through the stillness. He turned sharply, startled. A younger man stood there, panting, his eyes wide with panic.

"Go away," he snapped. "You don't even know me. What does it matter to you?"

"It matters because I'm here," the young man shot back. "I see you. And I don't want to watch you jump. Now get down."

He scoffed, shaking his head. "Just leave me alone."

The younger man pulled out his phone. "If you don't step away from that edge right now, I swear I'll call the police."

His heart pounded. He clenched his jaw. The last thing he needed was cops showing up, dragging him away like some lunatic. He hesitated, then begrudgingly took a step back. Instantly, the young man rushed forward, grabbing his arm and guiding him farther from the edge.

"Good," the younger man said, still holding onto him like he might make a run for it. "Now that I've ruined your plan, how about you get a cup of coffee with me?"

He snorted. "What?"

The younger man grinned, a bright, disarming smile. "Yeah, come on. One coffee. Humour me."

He hesitated. Then sighed. "Fine. One coffee."

As they sat in a quiet café, the younger man—Gus, as he introduced himself—kept up a steady stream of chatter.

"So, are you gonna tell me why you were up there?"

He stared into his cup. "Why does it matter to you so much? Are you a social worker or something?"

Gus shook his head. "Nope. Just a guy who saw another guy about to make a big mistake."

He scoffed. "Well, congratulations, you saved a life. Now you can sleep better at night."

Gus took a sip of his coffee, unfazed. "I don't want to 'save' you. I just want to understand."

A long silence stretched between them before he exhaled sharply, running a hand through his hair. "Fine. You wanna know?"

Gus nodded.

He let out a bitter laugh. "Lost my girlfriend of seven years. I kept messing things up, and she finally had enough. The house we were supposed to buy together? That's gone too. My job? Fired. I was supposed to be saving for a future, but all I've got left is enough to keep me afloat for a few months. My parents don't even want to talk to me. I'm a disappointment to them. And my friends? They've moved on. They have careers, marriages, kids—whole lives I'm not a part of anymore."

He clenched his jaw. "So, tell me, Gus. What exactly am I supposed to be looking forward to?"

Gus was quiet for a moment. Then, he leaned back in his chair and exhaled. "Damn. That's rough."

"No shit."

"I mean it," Gus said, stirring his coffee absentmindedly. "That's a lot for anyone. But... you know, it's not the end."

He gave Gus a tired look. "Spare me the 'it gets better' speech."

Gus smirked. "I wasn't gonna say that. I was gonna say, 'this sucks.' And I know because I've been there."

That caught him off guard. "What?"

Gus was quiet for a moment. Then, he leaned back in his chair and exhaled. "Well... what if it was all a lie?"

He frowned. "Huh? What do you mean?"

"What if you're just imagining things? What if you didn't mess up your relationship, and she's just waiting for you to call? What if your job firing you wasn't a loss, but a push toward something better? You admitted yourself that you were stagnant. What if this is the wake-up call you needed?"

He opened his mouth to argue, but Gus kept going. "Your parents—are they ashamed? Or are they just worried and hoping you'll find your way? And your friends? Have you even told them what you're going through? Maybe they're just unaware because you never reached out."

The words hit like a slap. He pushed back his chair, his face hardening. "I don't need solutions from a 22-year-old kid who doesn't even know me."

He stormed out.

But later, alone in his small rented apartment, Gus's words echoed in his mind. What if he had exaggerated everything in his frustration? He still couldn't bring himself to call his girlfriend, but that night, he updated his resume and started applying for jobs.

The next two weeks were filled with interviews and emails. Suddenly, he had a purpose again. One day, walking to an interview, he ran into an old friend.

"Hey, man! Where've you been?" his friend grinned. "Haven't seen you in ages."

"Nothing much... just been busy. I lost my job recently, so I've been looking for a new one."

His friend's face fell. "Dude, why didn't you tell me? I could've helped! We're friends for a reason. Do you need anything?"

He smiled, touched by the concern. "Nah, I'm good. Just heading to an interview."

"That's awesome! I'm coming with you!"

"Huh? You don't need to. Don't you have work?"

"Work can wait. Right now, my friend needs support. Let's go!"

As he walked back to his apartment after lunch, the realization struck him like a bolt of lightning.

What if Gus was right? What if, in his frustration, he had blown everything out of proportion? What if his own despair had clouded his judgment, making problems seem bigger than they were—blinding him to the solutions that had been there all along?

His breath quickened. His heart pounded. Without thinking, he turned around and ran. Ran through the busy streets, past people going about their lives, ignoring the burning in his legs, the racing of his pulse. He didn't stop until he was standing in front of her door. He knocked frantically. Seconds passed. The longest seconds of his life.

Then the door opened.

His breath caught at the sight of her—her tired, wary eyes, the hesitation in her expression. Before she could speak, the words spilled out. "I'm sorry." Her lips parted in shock. For a moment, she just stared at him. Then, suddenly, she let out a shaky breath—and before he knew it, tears welled in her eyes.

"You idiot," she whispered. And then, she was laughing and crying at the same time, covering her face with her hands.

His chest tightened. "I messed up," he admitted. "I—I let my frustration consume me. I took it all out on you. On us. And you didn't deserve that."

She wiped her tears, sniffling. "No, I didn't."

He nodded, swallowing hard. "But I need you to know... I never stopped loving you. Not for a second."

She exhaled shakily, looking up at him. "Then why did you push me away?"

"Because I felt like a failure," he admitted. "I lost my job. I had no future. I didn't know how to fix things, so I shut down. But that wasn't fair to you."

She searched his face, her gaze softening. "I never wanted to leave you."

His throat tightened. "I know."

Silence settled between them—heavy, yet full of unspoken understanding. Finally, he took a deep breath. "I've been applying for jobs. I have interviews lined up. I'm trying to fix things. And I don't expect you to forgive me right away, but... if you'll have me, I want to make things right." For a moment, she didn't move. Then, slowly, she stepped forward and wrapped her arms around him, burying her face in his shoulder. "Of course," she whispered again. "I promised to be with you through better or worse. I'm not going anywhere."

He let out a shaky laugh, hugging her tightly. They stayed like that for a long time.

The next morning, he took a deep breath and knocked on another door. His parents'. When his mother opened it, her expression flickered between surprise and hesitation. His father appeared behind her, arms crossed, face unreadable. They hadn't spoken in months. For a second, he wanted to turn back. But then he thought of Gus's words. "Have you even talked to them?"

So he stayed.

"Can we talk?" he asked.

His mother hesitated, then stepped aside. "Come in."

Inside, the air was tense. He could feel the weight of unspoken disappointment, the judgment he had imagined over and over.

But then, his father finally spoke. "Why now?"

His stomach twisted, but he met his father's gaze. "Because I want to know the truth," he admitted. "I want to know if you're really ashamed of me... or if I just assumed you were."

His father's eyes flickered with something unreadable.

"We were never ashamed of you," his mother said quietly. "We were worried."

His breath hitched. "Then why didn't you say anything?"

His father sighed. "Because we didn't know how. And because we wanted you to do better. We just... we didn't know if pushing you would help or hurt you."

He swallowed hard. "I felt like I was drowning."

"We know," his mother whispered. "And we're sorry we didn't reach out sooner."

A heavy silence followed. But for the first time, it wasn't suffocating. They talked for hours. And by the time he left, he realized something—his parents hadn't wanted to see him fail. They had wanted to see him rise.

The next day, he found himself outside the same building where everything had almost ended. He wasn't looking up at the rooftop this time. He was looking around, searching. And then—there he was. Gus. Sitting at the same café. This time, he was the one to approach. He placed two cups of coffee on the table and slid into the chair across from him. "You were right," he admitted. Gus smirked. "I usually am." He huffed a laugh. "I've been trying to get back on track. With my life. With my girlfriend. My parents. Everything." He picked up his coffee, staring into it. "It's not perfect, but I'm trying." Gus leaned back, nodding in approval. "That's all that matters."

For the first time, he didn't feel like a failure. He felt... hopeful.

The next six months weren't easy. He failed interviews. Lost opportunities. Faced rejection after rejection. But this time, he didn't break. Because he had people standing by him. Not as burdens, but as his support. As a reason to keep pushing forward. And then—finally—it happened. He landed a job. A real, stable, well-paying job. A job that allowed him to save again. Save for the future he thought he had lost.

A few months later, he bought a ring. And as he stood in front of his girlfriend—no, his 'fiancée'—watching her eyes light up with love and disbelief, he realized something. His life wasn't over. It had only just begun.

Then, one day, he went looking for Gus, wanting to ask him to be his best man. He waited at the coffee shop, and finally, Gus arrived.

He slid a cup of coffee across the table. "My treat," he said with a small grin.

Gus raised an eyebrow but accepted it. "So," he mused, "what's next for you?"

He exhaled, leaning back in his chair. "Keep moving forward. One step at a time."

Gus studied him for a moment, then nodded in approval.

After a beat of silence, he asked, "Why did you help me that day?"

Gus shrugged. "A couple years ago, I was in a bad place too. Different reasons, but the same feeling—like I had nothing left. I know what it's like to think there's no way out."

He frowned slightly, searching Gus's face for any sign of insincerity. He found none. "So what changed?"

Gus sighed, a small, knowing smile tugging at his lips. "Someone sat down and had coffee with me."

For the first time, something in his chest eased.

He looked down at his coffee, the steam curling into the air, and thought,

"Maybe... just maybe... I'll stick around for another cup."

Before he could ask him to be his best-man, the waitress called his coffee order. He turned for just a second.

When he turned back—Gus was gone. His brows furrowed. He looked around the café, scanning every table, every corner. Nothing. A strange unease settled in his stomach. He turned to the waitress. "Did you see where the guy I was sitting with went?"

She blinked. "Who?"

"The guy sitting right here. Gus."

She gave him a puzzled look. "Sir, you came in alone."

His breath caught. "No, I—I was just talking to him. Right here."

But when he turned to the other customers, they only shrugged. No one had seen Gus.

A slow dread crept through his veins. He rushed to the café manager. "Can I check the security footage?" His voice was barely steady.

Minutes later, he watched the screen. There he was—walking in alone. Sitting alone. Talking to... no one. His heart pounded in his chest. This couldn't be right. Gus 'was real'. He had to be. He stumbled out of the café, his mind racing.

At home, he told his fiancée everything. She listened, eyes filled with quiet concern, until something seemed to click in her mind. She hesitated, then asked, "Wasn't your nickname Gus in high school?" His stomach dropped. She pulled out an old photo album, flipping through the pages until she landed on a picture of him from years ago. "And... the way you described him. He looks exactly like you did back then." His pulse roared in his ears as he stared at the photo.

Gus was him.

It had always been him. Memories rushed back—the way Gus had known exactly what to say, the way no one else had acknowledged him, the way he had pushed him forward when no one else could.

It hadn't been a stranger who saved him that day on the rooftop.

III

Stochastic Process

Dr. Elara Voss had spent years studying stochastic processes—the mathematical framework used to model systems that evolve with randomness. She believed the universe was not deterministic but a complex web of probabilities, where turning points—critical, finite-dimensional moments—dictated the trajectory of reality. Her work aimed to quantify these moments, to isolate the exact mathematical set that caused one reality to emerge from an ocean of possibilities.

And now, she was using that very research to go back in time. Not to change anything. Just to understand.

No matter how many equations she derived, models she ran, or variables she replayed, she couldn't pinpoint the precise cause of this reality—why Nathan left. Why, out of all possible outcomes, this was the one she was living.

Her fingers trembled as she adjusted the device strapped to her wrist. The culmination of years of research—refined to transport her consciousness back to a single moment, the same moment, over and over. A closed system, an isolated equation. She had assumed the cause was simple: she hadn't shown up for dinner, and that was the fracture point. But her models told her otherwise.

Elara was used to finding patterns in chaos. She had built her entire career on it.

But standing in the middle of her old lab, watching her past-self ignore Nathan's message, she felt completely blind.

There was always more than one variable in play. She exhaled, bracing herself, then activated the device.

Time unravelled.

She landed in her lab on the night of the dinner.

The air smelled of coffee and whiteboard markers, just as she remembered. Papers were scattered across the desk, dense with equations, half-erased diagrams filling every whiteboard. The hum of the overhead lights and the faint whir of her computer's cooling fan settled around her like a ghost of a life she no longer inhabited.

Her past-self sat hunched over the desk, scribbling frantically, lips moving as she worked through a proof. The clock on the wall read 7:42 PM. Nathan had been waiting at the restaurant since 7:30.

Elara exhaled, steadying herself. She had been here before. Over and over. Each time, she watched the same series of events unfold like a well-rehearsed play. Her past self, utterly engrossed in research. The phone buzzing. The absentminded glance. The dismissal. The moment that sealed her fate.

She stepped forward cautiously.

'Why didn't you just look at your phone?'

The data suggested that her absence that night had an 82% probability weight in causing the breakup. A staggering number. But not 100%. And that gap, that missing 18%, gnawed at her.

She pulled out her tablet and reran the simulation for the hundredth time. A three-dimensional projection of past events unfolded before her, variables mapped in glowing lines of probability. Her device reconstructed reality based on known information, filling in details based on data extrapolation.

Her past-self sat hunched at the desk, scribbling equations. Then came the familiar sound. A short, vibrating buzz against the desk. Nathan's message.

Her past-self picked up the phone, read the text. "Been waiting since 7:30. Are you coming?"

A flicker of hesitation. Barely a second. Then she placed the phone face-down without responding.

"I'll make it up to him tomorrow," past Elara whispered under her breath.

Present Elara clenched her fists.

'You never did.'

She had seen this before. But this time, she wasn't here to wallow in regret. She was here to isolate the finite-dimensional turning point—the precise variable that made this outcome inevitable.

She adjusted the wrist device, activating a real-time analysis of the room's information density. It filtered unnecessary data, highlighting only the variables with the highest probability contribution to the outcome.

Nathan's message lit up in the projection.

Again. Again. Again. 'Come on, think.'

She adjusted the parameters. Removed redundant data. If there was an anomaly, she would find it.

Except... there was nothing new. Her hands tightened into fists.

It has to be here.

She stepped closer to the projected model, scanning for unaccounted data points. Time pulsed around her in a slow loop, replaying the same thirty minutes over and over. Every possible factor was accounted for.

Or so she thought.

She adjusted her wrist device to expand the data parameters. Her algorithm could only process so much at once—perhaps she had set the filtering constraints too tight. If she removed all assumptions about what mattered and let the raw data speak for itself, maybe...

A new variable flickered into view. A second notification.

Node Identified: Primary Event – Non-Response to Communication (Weight: 82%)

Yes, she already knew that. But why? What unseen variable had made her miss the dinner that night?

She recalibrated, expanding the information field. The algorithm sifted through environmental factors, emotional state fluctuations, subconscious behaviours—searching for anomalies.

Then—a fluctuation.

A ripple in the data. A hidden variable buried within the noise.

She frowned. She had run this analysis before and never found this distortion. She refined the parameters, isolating the source of the inconsistency.

It wasn't Nathan's message. It was something else.

A second notification had arrived at almost the exact same moment. But her past selves had ignored it completely.

Elara's breath hitched. That wasn't in any of her previous observations. She had assumed she had accounted for all possible factors. But this was something new. Something she had overlooked.

She frowned. "What is this?"

That didn't make sense. She had never noticed a second notification before. She let the simulation run again, this time watching more carefully.

At 7:39 PM, her phone had buzzed twice in succession.

The first was Nathan's message. The second—

Elara narrowed her eyes.

The second had come from an unknown number.

A single unread message.

"See you tonight. Can't wait. ♥?"

She adjusted the frequency to extract the metadata. The message's timestamp sat uncomfortably close to Nathan's. Minutes apart.

Elara's heart pounded. She had spent months thinking the dinner was the cause. That it was her fault. But now, something else was shifting into focus.

She adjusted her device again. One more time.

She arrived in a different moment. Not in her lab.

Not in the restaurant.

Outside their apartment. The night of the dinner.

This was risky. She had never gone back to this point in time before—there were too many unknowns, too many variables that could disrupt the system. Her research had always focused on her role in the breakup, so she had never tried observing Nathan's side of the timeline.

Now, she had to.

From the shadows of the street, she watched as Nathan paced by the window, his face illuminated by the glow of his phone screen. His fingers moved in deliberate strokes, typing. Pausing. Deleting. Rewriting. His expression was unreadable. He typed something, then hesitated, his thumb hovering over the screen.

A moment later, he pressed send.

Elara didn't need to check. She knew what it was.

Elara held her breath. She braced herself, waiting for his next move. She had replayed this moment endlessly, believing this was the axis upon which everything turned. But now, she wasn't so sure.

Then, the doorbell rang.

Nathan stilled. Nathan set his phone down on the counter without a second thought and walked to the door.

A woman stepped inside. Smiling. Familiar. Comfortable.

Elara's stomach twisted into a knot and felt the air leave her lungs.

The way she moved. The way she smiled at Nathan as if she belonged there. Nathan didn't hesitate. He leaned in, pressing a kiss to the woman's lips with the ease of someone who had done it before. Not rushed. Not uncertain. This wasn't new.

Elara staggered back, mind whirling.

Her missing dinner wasn't the turning point—it, it was never about the dinner. It was just the final piece he needed to make it look like it was her fault.

He had already decided to leave. He had already replaced her. She just hadn't known.

She had spent months blaming herself. Days believing she had made the wrong choice, that she had miscalculated, that she had let the wrong set of variables dictate the future.

But the equation had never been balanced. There had always been an external force acting upon the system—one she had never observed, never accounted for.

She had spent years trying to model a closed system, believing she could isolate a finite-dimensional set of factors that led to a single, inevitable conclusion. But she had been wrong. The system was never closed. There were external forces she had never observed, never accounted for. Nathan's decisions, his betrayals—they were variables outside her field of study.

She activated the device. Time collapsed once again.

She returned to the present, sitting alone in her dimly lit lab. The equations on the board blurred as she stared through them. Her hands trembled.

It wasn't her.

It wasn't her fault. But that didn't make her feel better.

Her entire identity had been built on the idea that the world—her world—could be explained, predicted, controlled. That everything could be traced back to some finite-dimensional set, some quantifiable moment in time that dictated the outcome.

But a small, insidious voice in the back of her mind whispered: Wasn't it, though?

She had been absent. Distracted. She had prioritized her research over him, over their relationship, over the life they were supposed to build together.

"Maybe if you had been home more, this wouldn't have happened."

"Maybe if you had paid more attention, you would have seen the signs."

"Maybe it was still your fault."

Would he have cheated if she had been more present? If she had come home earlier, reached for him in the night instead of reaching for her notebook? If she had put down her research—just for a moment—and looked at him like she used to?

But then, another thought emerged. One colder. Sharper.

"No."

"I spent years thinking I was the one who failed."

Nathan hadn't left because she missed one dinner. He hadn't left because she worked too much. He left because he wanted to.

He had made his choice long before that night. He had been waiting for the right moment, the right excuse, to walk away clean. And she had given it to him, wrapped in guilt, neatly absolving him of responsibility.

A bitter laugh escaped her lips. She had spent so much time trying to solve her heartbreak, trying to break it down into quantifiable steps, as if grief could be mapped onto an equation.

But this wasn't math. This wasn't science. This was just human nature, chaotic and untraceable. She had her answer now. She wiped a hand down her face, feeling the weight of exhaustion settle in.

For months, she had been trapped in a recursive loop, replaying the past, trying to rewrite the narrative in her mind, searching for the moment that would justify her regret.

But there was no equation that could change the past. And no amount of math or theory could explain why some people stay and others leave. No formula that could turn back time and make someone stay. Her gaze flicked to the wrist device, sitting silent beside her. For the first time, she felt no urge to use it.

She exhaled, then picked up a marker and turned back to her work. If she couldn't control the past, she would control the future.

Her research would move forward. She would prove her theories. She would present her findings to the world. Nathan was just one outcome in a stochastic process—a path that had collapsed into reality, but not the only one.

And she still had infinite possibilities ahead.

IV

Mothers & Daughters

The kitchen smelled of cinnamon and warm butter as Ria rolled out the dough, and her mother, Paro, walked beside her, guiding her hands when necessary. The late evening sun streamed through the window, casting a golden glow over them. The rhythmic sound of the rolling pin against the wooden counter filled the space, a comforting melody of familiarity.

"You're doing good," Paro said, smiling softly as she watched Ria press down on the dough with determination.

Ria smirked. "You always say that even when I mess up."

Paro chuckled, shaking her head. "Because enjoying the process matters more than rushing through it. And besides, sometimes when you slow down, you notice things you never saw before."

Ria considered that then shrugged. "I guess that makes sense."

They sat in silence for a moment, the air between them thick with unspoken thoughts. The record crackled softly in the background, the melody weaving through the quiet. Ria absentmindedly ran her fingers over a faded photograph of a younger Paro, her eyes alight with unspoken dreams.

Finally, Ria asked, her voice quieter now, "Mom... was it hard? Raising me?"

Paro exhaled, closing the album for a moment as if the pull of the memories had suddenly become too much. She studied Ria's face—the sharp determination in her gaze, the quiet strength in the set of her jaw. So much of herself reflected, yet Ria carried something of her own too—a softness, a hopefulness Paro once had but had long buried under responsibility.

"Raising a daughter is... different. Not harder, just different. The world has expectations of girls that it doesn't have for boys. I had to teach you how to stand your ground with grace, to be fierce yet compassionate, to trust your intuition but also demand respect. How to be strong without losing your tenderness, how to be independent yet know when to lean on others. How to be kind without being taken for granted. How to dream fearlessly but also navigate reality with wisdom and resilience."

Ria traced a finger over a photo of Paro in her twenties, laughing in a sunlit park. "That sounds... exhausting."

Paro smiled wistfully, the weight of years reflected in her eyes. "It was. Some days, it felt like I was struggling against things no one else could see—fear, doubt, a world that tried to shape you before you even knew yourself. But it was also the most important thing I've ever done. Every moment, every sacrifice, every lesson—I did it so you could have more than I did. So you could move through life without the same obstacles I had to overcome."

Ria tilted her head. "Like what?"

Paro's gaze drifted toward the window as if looking back at her past. "Opportunities. Freedom. Choices. I had dreams, you know. Big ones. I wanted to travel, to see the world beyond this town. I wanted to paint, to create something that would last longer than me. But life... life has a way of rearranging your priorities."

Ria frowned. "Do you regret it?"

Paro's fingers traced the pages of the old album, her gaze distant, as if looking back at the choices that had shaped her. "Regret?" she murmured, rolling the word over as if testing its gravity. "No. I made my choices with love, with duty, with hope. But sometimes... sometimes I wonder."

She glanced at Ria, a bittersweet smile playing on her lips. "I wonder who I might have been if I had chosen differently. If I had been a little braver, a little more selfish. If I had chased my dreams instead of waiting for the right time—because the right time never really comes, does it?"

Ria swallowed, watching the depth of unspoken stories flicker in Paro's eyes. "But you're happy now, aren't you?"

Paro's smile softened. "Happiness isn't always about what we get—it's about what we make of what we have. And I have a lot to be grateful for." She reached across the table, squeezing Ria's hand. "But if you ever find yourself standing at a door you want to walk through—promise me you won't wait."

Ria watched her mother carefully. "Do you ever wish you had chosen differently?"

Paro turned to her, her eyes soft but certain. "No. Not for a second. Because every road I took, every sacrifice I made, led me here—to you. And you, Ria, are the best thing I've ever done. But just because I made sacrifices doesn't mean you have to make the same ones. I want you to have choices, and to chase every dream without hesitation. I want you to go after everything you want, not just what feels safe or expected. I want you to live without regret."

Ria swallowed, the impact of her mother's words settling deep in her chest. "But what if I don't know exactly what I want yet?"

Paro smiled, brushing a strand of hair from Ria's face, her touch gentle yet firm. "Then that's the beauty of it, isn't it? You don't have to have all the answers right now. You just have to give yourself the freedom to find them. Take your time. Explore. Make mistakes. Change your mind a hundred times if you need to. Just promise me you'll never let fear or doubt decide for you. That's the only way you'll ever truly be free"

She turned back to the album in her lap, her fingers gliding over a faded photograph. "When I was your age, I thought I had to have everything figured out. I thought I had to choose one path and never look back. But life... life doesn't work like that. It twists and turns. It surprises you. And sometimes, the things you think you want to change along the way."

Ria bit her lip. "But what if I make the wrong choice?"

Paro's eyes met hers, filled with a quiet, unwavering love. "Then you learn from it. You adjust. You move forward. No choice is ever truly wrong if it teaches you something. But don't let fear keep you from making one at all."

She squeezed Ria's hand, her voice softer now, but no less certain. "Just promise me one thing—when you stand at a crossroads, don't pick the safest route just because it's familiar. Be brave enough to choose the one that excites you, even if it scares you. That's how you build a life without regret."

Ria nodded slowly, feeling something shift inside her—a tiny spark of courage, of possibility. Maybe she didn't have all the answers yet. But for the first time, that didn't feel so terrifying.

Ria frowned, her voice quiet. "But, Ma... I want to be like you."

Paro blinked, surprised. "Like me?"

"Yeah." Ria turned to face her fully now, her eyes steady with conviction. "You say there were things you didn't get to do, but look at you. You stand firm in who you are. You don't let anyone else define you. You hold onto what matters, even when it's difficult—even when you're standing alone. You take care of me, of everyone around you, without ever asking for anything in return."

You built this life for us by yourself, from the ground up. When things got tough, you didn't break—you held on, you figured it out. You never waited for someone else to rescue you, because you knew you could do it yourself. And you did. You proved that strength isn't just about being tough—it's about resilience, about love, about standing tall even when the world tries to push you down.

"That's the kind of woman I want to be—not just brave, but steadfast. Not just independent, but sure of who I am. I want to be like you, Mom. Because if I can carry even a piece of the strength and grace you have, I'll know I'm on the right path."

Paro felt a lump rise in her throat, the sudden surge of emotion catching her off guard. But as she looked at Ria now—her daughter, her greatest achievement—she realized those fears had been unfounded.

Ria didn't see her as a cautionary tale. She saw her as a foundation. A woman who had stood tall despite life's storms. A woman who had loved fiercely, given selflessly, and never once let the hardships of the world break her.

Paro exhaled, her fingers tightening around the worn pages of the album in her lap. "I used to wonder," she admitted, her voice softer now, "if you'd look at my life and see only what slipped away—the dreams I had to set aside, the struggles I faced alone. I worried you'd think that standing tall meant losing too much."

Ria's expression softened, her brows drawing together in something like understanding. "I don't see loss when I look at you, Ma. I see strength. I see a woman who never stopped pushing forward. I see a woman who kept going, even when life tested her at every turn. Someone who carried her responsibilities with grace, who gave her all without ever letting the world define her. I see resilience—not in the loud, obvious ways, but in the quiet moments, in the love you poured into our lives and every crack until it became something unbreakable, in the way you never let hardship harden you. You didn't just push through, Ma. You built something beautiful. I see love, determination, and a spirit that never faded, no matter how much the world tried to quiet it."

Paro swallowed against the lump in her throat, overwhelmed by the certainty in Ria's voice. Had she really done that? Had she really given her daughter more than just cautionary tales?

Ria reached across the table, covering Paro's hand with her own. "You didn't teach me that strength comes at too high a cost. You taught me that strength is knowing what's worth fighting for. That love, family, and dreams don't have to be separate things. And most of all, you taught me that no matter how life twists and turns, we always have the power to choose what comes next."

But now, hearing this, it was as if every late night spent worrying, every tear shed in private, every moment of doubt had transformed into something meaningful. Ria didn't see a woman burdened by the past; she saw someone who had risen above it. Every hardship, every sacrifice, every moment Paro had spent forging ahead despite the odds—it all led to this.

Tears burned at Paro's eyes, but she let them fall, for once not bothering to hold them back. Because at that moment, she knew—her sacrifices had never been in vain. Her daughter didn't just understand her. She saw her.

Paro's breath hitched, the force of Ria's words settling deep in her chest. For so long, she had measured her life in the things she had given up, the dreams she had tucked away in quiet corners of her heart. But hearing Ria now, she realized—her daughter had never seen a loss in her story.

She reached over, fingers brushing against Ria's cheek before tucking a stray strand of hair behind her ear. "You already are," she murmured, a small, bittersweet smile tugging at her lips. "You have a light in you, Ria—bright, steady, and all your own. But I want more for you than just strength—I want you to have choices. The kind I didn't always have. I want you to chase happiness without second-guessing, to build a life that's truly yours. Courage matters, but so does the freedom to be soft when you choose to be. To love without fear, to take risks, to fall and trust that you'll find your way again. You don't have to carry every burden—you just have to live in a way that feels true to you."

Paro let out a shaky breath, her fingers tightening around Ria's. Maybe she had spent too long mourning the roads she never took. Maybe, all along, she had been looking at her life through the wrong lens. Because if this—this fierce, kind, brilliant daughter sitting before her—was the result of every choice she had made, then how could she ever call them regrets?

Paro smiled, warmth filling her chest, her heart full in a way she hadn't expected. "And you are everything I dreamed you'd be—and more. You're strong, yes, but you also have something I fought so hard to hold on to. Hope. A belief that the world can be yours, that you don't have to choose between strength and softness, between independence and love. That's what I always wanted for you."

The oven timer dinged, a small but fitting reminder that time never stops, not even for moments like these. Paro laughed, ruffling Ria's hair as she wiped at the corner of her eye. "Alright, let's see if these cookies survived our little heart-to-heart. Though I think we just proved something more important—you've already got all the right ingredients to be whoever you want to be."

Ria grinned, nudging Paro playfully. "With you teaching me? They'll be perfect. Just like you."

Paro scoffed, but there was warmth in her eyes as she pulled the tray from the oven, the rich scent of cinnamon and sugar curling into the air. She set it on the counter, tapping a finger against the edge as she glanced at Ria. "I like that confidence," she said, a teasing lilt in her voice. "And you know what? Maybe I did raise you right after all."

Ria leaned against the counter, watching her mother carefully lift each cookie onto a plate. It was such a small moment, an ordinary one, yet something about it felt profound—like a quiet kind of love, steady and unwavering, woven into the simple act of baking together.

She picked up a warm cookie, breaking it in half, and offering a piece to Paro. "You didn't just raise me right,

Mom," she murmured. "You raised me capable. You raised me loved."

Paro stilled for a moment, then smiled—soft, knowing, full of something unspoken yet deeply understood. She took the offered piece, shaking her head with a mock sigh. "Alright, alright. Now stop before you make me cry. Eat your cookies before they get cold."

But as they stood there, side by side, the scent of cinnamon wrapping around them like an embrace, Ria knew—this moment, this warmth, this love—was something she'd carry with her forever.

V

Like, follow and share

Ash sat on her balcony, her arms wrapped around her knees as she stared out at the city lights. Below her, the world pulsed with life—cars honking, neon signs flickering, people laughing in the streets. It was beautiful, chaotic, real. Yet she felt like a ghost, trapped in the space between the world she longed for and the one she had been taught to live in.

The night air was cool against her skin, carrying with it the hum of the city below. Her mind wandered to the past, to a time before she had been consumed by the virtual world, before her life became curated by what she posted and how many likes she received.

She used to think the world was simple. People were kind, honest, good. At least, that's what she had always believed. But the older she got, the more people told her she was wrong. They said she was naive, that she needed to understand people's real intentions. They told her to stop being so trusting, to look past smiles and see what lay beneath. But Lena couldn't. She had read about betrayal, manipulation, cruelty—but reading was different from believing. She couldn't imagine people truly being that twisted. And because of that, she struggled.

Conversations confused her. A joke could carry venom, a compliment could be a trap, a friend could be an enemy in disguise. The rules weren't written down, and no one would explain them to her. They only told her to "see things for what they were," as if that was something easy to do. So, eventually, she stopped asking. She stopped speaking much at all.

And it was worse online. Social media had perfected the art of illusion. She would scroll past hundreds of posts—perfect vacations, glowing skin, six-figure salaries, and effortless success. It was all so polished, so carefully curated. Even the struggles that people shared felt scripted, as if hardship itself had become another performance. The "rags to riches" story was everywhere, repeated by different faces but always following the same arc, the same neatly-packaged inspiration. It no longer felt real. It felt like just another product to consume.

She used to believe failure was a personal journey. You fell, you made mistakes, and you learned. You figured things out through trial and error, through experience, through actually living. But now? Now there were thousands of voices telling her what to do, step by step, in bite-sized videos. "Wake up at 5 AM." "Read these ten books." "Follow this morning routine for success." It was endless, exhausting, and impersonal.

How were you supposed to find your own way when you were constantly being told what your way should be?

The more advice she consumed, the more stuck she felt. Every path had been walked before, every lesson already distilled into an aesthetic infographic. It was paralyzing. She was supposed to be inspired, but instead, she felt lost.

She whispered to herself, "When did we stop figuring things out for ourselves? When did we start believing that the only way to succeed was to follow someone else's script?"

Her mind answered immediately. "When we stopped trusting ourselves. When we started thinking that someone out there had the perfect formula."

She exhaled sharply. "But there is no perfect formula to life. Not really. There's just... life and living."

She would stare at her screen, watching people achieve things she didn't even want, yet still feeling like she was falling behind. Someone was getting an award, someone else was starting a company, another was traveling the world, another buying their first home. It wasn't even about envy—it wasn't that she wanted those things for herself. But somehow, seeing them, seeing everyone moving forward while she remained stagnant, made her feel like she was failing at something. Even if she didn't know what.

She started questioning herself. What was she doing with her life? Was she wasting time? Should she be chasing something more? But more of what? She didn't even know what she wanted. All she knew was that whatever she was doing, it wasn't enough.

Every time she looked in the mirror, she saw someone who wasn't achieving anything. Just a girl standing still while the world moved around her. The notifications on her phone—likes, comments, messages—those weren't her. They were just echoes of interaction, shallow and fleeting. They weren't accomplishments, they weren't real growth.

They were just pixels on a screen, keeping her tethered to a world that wasn't even hers.

She whispered to herself, "Why do I care? Why does it feel like I'm failing at a race I never even signed up for?"

Her reflection didn't have an answer. It just stared back, tired and uncertain.

She used to run through the neighbourhood streets barefoot, feeling the heat of the pavement in the summer. She used to climb trees, not caring about the dirt on her hands, the scratches on her legs. As a child, the world was something to be touched, felt, experienced without hesitation. There were no filters, no angles, no perfect lighting—just the moment, raw and real.

Her first interaction with social media had been innocent enough. A friend had introduced her to it in middle school. It started with simple posts—pictures of her cat, snapshots of family trips. She never cared about how many people saw them; she just liked sharing things she found beautiful. But that changed. Slowly, the numbers started to matter. How many likes. How many comments. How many followers.

By high school, she was trapped in it. The pressure to present a perfect version of herself had crept in so subtly she hadn't even noticed. It wasn't enough to just exist anymore—she had to be seen, validated, admired. Her friends all played the game, some better than others. The ones who knew the rules thrived. The ones who didn't, like her, got lost.

She remembered the first time someone had laughed at a picture she posted, not because it was funny, but because it wasn't "good enough."

"Ugh, Lena, the lighting is so weird in this," her friend Emily had said, squinting at the screen. "And your face looks kinda... awkward?"

"Yeah," another chimed in, "Maybe try taking it again, like from this angle?"

Lena had felt a knot form in her stomach. She had liked that picture. It was just a simple selfie, nothing special, but now, suddenly, it wasn't right. She had taken out her phone and tried again. And again.

"How's this one?" she had asked hesitantly, showing them.

Emily studied it and nodded. "Better. But maybe a filter? Something warmer."

Lena had applied the filter, smoothed her skin, adjusted the brightness. It still wasn't perfect, but she uploaded it anyway.

When the likes didn't come as expected, she had stared at the screen, refreshing, waiting. The number stayed disappointingly low. Her stomach sank.

"Maybe delete it," she had muttered to herself. And she did. As if it had never existed.

That was the beginning. From that moment on, she didn't just take pictures. She curated them. She posed, adjusted, analyzed. It was no longer about sharing something she loved—it was about getting it right. And "right" wasn't even something she could define. It was whatever got the most approval, the most engagement.

It wasn't just about pictures. It was about everything. The way she spoke, the things she liked, even the way she thought. Everything had to be tailored, adjusted, optimized. And somewhere along the way, she had stopped recognizing herself.

Her parents didn't understand.

"Just put your phone down," her mother would say, shaking her head as she wiped down the kitchen counter.

"You spend too much time staring at that thing."

"It's not that easy," Lena would reply, her voice laced with frustration.

"Why not?" her father chimed in from across the room. "When we were your age, we didn't need any of that."

Lena let out a bitter laugh. "Yeah, well, when you were my age, people weren't measuring their worth in likes and engagement rates."

She closed her eyes and leaned her head back against the chair. When had it gotten this bad? When had she stopped living for herself?

She whispered now, staring at the city, "When did I start living for an audience instead of myself?"

She remembered a time when she didn't care how she looked in photos, when she laughed without wondering if it would look good on camera. When she did things just because they made her happy, not because they would make good content.

"I miss that girl," she murmured to herself.

The past felt like a different lifetime. She could still see herself, a little girl with scraped knees, laughing under the sun. She had been real once. And now? Now she was tired.

Her phone buzzed beside her, pulling her back. She glanced at it but didn't pick it up. It could wait. For once, the world inside the screen wasn't the one she wanted to be in.

She sighed and muttered to herself, "Why do I do this? Why do I care so much about people who don't even know me?"

Her mind answered immediately. "Because they made you believe you had to. That your worth is tied to their approval."

She rubbed her temples. "That's ridiculous. I'm not just some profile picture, some perfectly edited highlight reel.

I'm a person. Right?"

Silence. The kind that left a heavy, sinking feeling in her gut.

"Then why do I feel like I don't know who that person is anymore?" she whispered.

She scrolled less and less. At first, it was unintentional—forgetting to post one day, skipping through stories without really looking. Then it became deliberate. She avoided the feed, ignored notifications, let messages go unanswered. Eventually, she deleted the apps entirely.

At first, it felt strange, like a phantom limb. Her fingers would instinctively reach for her phone, scrolling through empty screens before realizing there was nothing left to check. But as the days passed, the silence became a relief. The endless stream of content, the pressure to keep up, the subtle competition of who was living the most aesthetic life—it all started to feel so distant, like a dream she had finally woken up from.

Social media had been a mirror maze, an illusion where everyone carefully crafted their own reflections, showing only what they wanted the world to see. It was impossible to tell what was real and what was performance, and somewhere in that distortion, she had lost herself. She had spent so long trying to fit into a version of life that wasn't even hers, measuring her worth by numbers on a screen, seeking validation from people who didn't truly know her.

And for what? A fleeting sense of approval? The rush of a like, a comment, a repost? The exhaustion of trying to keep up had drained her. She had documented so much, but experienced so little.

She didn't want to live through a lens anymore. She didn't want to stage moments or filter them into something more appealing. She wanted to feel the wind on her skin without worrying if her hair looked right. She wanted to watch a sunset without thinking about how it would look on her profile.

A breeze drifted through the balcony, carrying the faint sounds of the city below. People were out there, living. Not posting, not performing—just existing. And she wanted that. She looked at the people below, walking freely through the streets, their laughter real and unedited. She wanted that. Not a perfectly structured five-step plan for happiness. Just the real, unfiltered experience of life—mistakes, uncertainty, and all.

I've expanded the scene, adding more depth to Lena's emotions, her longing for real life, and her internal struggle with breaking free from social media.

Tonight, as she looked down at the glowing streets, she longed to be there. Not just watching from above, but really there—walking down the sidewalks, breathing in the night air, experiencing life firsthand. She didn't want to think about angles, filters, or captions. She didn't want to measure the worth of a moment by how many people approved of it.

If she took a picture, it would be for herself. A memory, not a performance.

She drew her knees to her chest, holding herself tightly, the city lights flickering like stars below her. The world moved on without her, people laughing, cars honking, restaurants filled with chatter and music. A version of her used to be part of it. A version of her used to live.

"I used to be part of this," she whispered, the words barely escaping her lips. "I used to live in it, not just watch it. I want that back."

Her fingers twitched toward her phone. The habit was so ingrained, so automatic. A part of her wanted to check—just for a second. To scroll through the curated lives of people who barely knew she existed. To see what they were doing, what she was missing.

But wasn't that the problem? She wasn't missing anything. She was just existing on the edges of something that had never really been real.

She let her fingers brush over the cool glass of her phone but didn't pick it up.

Not tonight.

Maybe not ever.

She closed her eyes and took a deep breath, listening to the hum of the city. For the first time in a long time, she wanted to be here—not online, not lost in a screen, but here. Alive.

VI

Hated You

The first time I saw Sam Carter, I knew I hated him. It wasn't just a mild annoyance—it was the kind of deep, instinctual hatred that made my blood boil. He was arrogant, rude, and worst of all, dating my friend, Emily.

It wasn't that I liked him for myself. God, no. He just had this irritating way of acting like he owned the world, like he was better than everyone else. His confidence wasn't just confidence—it was the kind that made you want to roll your eyes so hard they'd get stuck.

We weren't even in the same class, but that didn't stop him from being a constant presence in my life. Every time I went to meet Emily, there he was, sitting on her desk like it was his personal throne, flashing that insufferable smirk like he knew something I didn't. And every single time, without fail, we'd end up bickering over the dumbest things.

Our fights were legendary. If I said the sky was blue, he'd insist it was gray. If I liked a song, he'd call it trash. If I breathed too loudly, he'd tell me to keep it down. It was a never-ending war of snarky comments and dramatic eye rolls.

"You are insufferable," I muttered one afternoon when he deliberately knocked my book off the desk.

"And you're a walking disaster," he shot back with a smirk.

One time, I was drinking a milkshake, minding my own business, when Sam casually strolled by and said, "Strawberry? Wow. Didn't take you for someone with the taste buds of a five-year-old."

I nearly threw the whole thing at him.

Another time, I tripped over a chair in Emily's classroom (grace has never been my strong suit), and before I could even recover, Sam had leaned in with that signature smirk and muttered, "And here I thought disasters were unpredictable. You? You're a guaranteed mess."

To which I snapped back, "And you? You're a guaranteed pain in my—"

Emily, who was stuck between us both, sighed. "Do you guys ever get tired of this?"

"No," we both answered at the same time, shooting each other glares.

No. No, we could not.

Because for some reason, Sam Carter existed solely to push my buttons, and I had made it my personal mission in life to push his right back.

One time, it got so bad that I ended up tearing his blazer during a particularly heated fight. He had made some snide comment about how I was "always causing trouble," and in my frustration, I grabbed his blazer to shove him back—except instead of just shoving him, I accidentally tore the sleeve.

Sam looked at me in pure horror. "You ripped my blazer?"

I blinked at the torn fabric in my hands. "Uh... whoops?"

"Whoops? This thing cost a fortune!"

"Well, maybe don't be so annoying next time." I crossed my arms, trying to hide the fact that I actually felt a little guilty.

He groaned. "You are the worst."

Emily just covered her face with her hands. "I can't tolerate you two together."

It happened on a cold evening in October. I had stayed back late at school for a club meeting. By the time I left, the hallways were deserted, and outside, the streets were quiet.

I had just turned a corner when I realized I wasn't alone. A group of three guys stood at the alley entrance, their faces shadowed under dim streetlights. My stomach clenched. I wasn't the type to get scared easily, but something about them set off alarms in my head.

"Hey, sweetheart," one of them called. "Walking alone?"

I turned around, trying to act casual, but my heart was pounding. "I'm just heading home."

One of them stepped forward, blocking my path. "Why don't you stay a little longer? We could use some company."

Panic shot through me. My hands clenched into fists. My phone was dead—just my luck. I braced myself to run, but before I could move, a voice rang out behind me.

"Hey! Get the hell away from her."

Sam.

I had never been so relieved to hear his voice. He stormed toward us, his usual smirk replaced with pure fury. "Didn't you hear me?" he growled. "Back off."

One of the guys scoffed. "And what are you gonna do about it?"

Sam didn't even hesitate. He stepped between me and them, his posture rigid, eyes burning with a dangerous intensity I had never seen before. "You don't want to find out," he said darkly.

There was something so certain about the way he stood, so unwavering, that even I felt a sense of security despite the situation. The three guys exchanged glances, clearly weighing their options. The tension in the air was suffocating. One of them muttered something under his breath, then jerked his chin at the others before they turned and walked away.

I let out a breath I hadn't realized I was holding, my hands still trembling slightly. The rush of adrenaline made my knees feel weak.

Sam turned to me, his expression still serious. "Are you okay?"

I swallowed hard and nodded. "Yeah. Thanks to you."

For a moment, there was silence. Then I blurted out, "Why did you help me? I thought you hated me."

Sam scoffed, running a hand through his messy hair. "Well, I do." He rolled his eyes before looking at me again, this time with something softer in his gaze. "But only I can hate you. You're my sister."

I blinked. "Excuse me?"

"You heard me." He crossed his arms. "I've spent too much time arguing with you to let some idiots mess with you. If anyone's going to make your life miserable, it's me."

Something in my chest tightened—but in a way that felt strangely warm, like the flicker of a candle in a dark room. For the first time, I saw him differently. He wasn't just Emily's annoying boyfriend, the guy I loved to argue with over the smallest things. He was someone who had my back, someone who—despite the relentless teasing—cared.

I stared at him, my mind trying to catch up with the moment. There was no sarcasm in his voice, no smug smirk playing at his lips. Just quiet sincerity. He meant it.

The weight of his words settled between us, heavy and unfamiliar. Before I could find something—anything—to say, he let out a sigh and nudged my shoulder lightly, as if sensing the tension. "Don't get all emotional on me, disaster," he muttered, shaking his head. "Let's get you home before you do something dumb again."

I rolled my eyes, the usual instinct to argue kicking in. But beneath it, something softer stirred. A quiet kind of gratitude. A reluctant fondness I wasn't quite ready to name.

"Fine," I huffed, crossing my arms. "But you still owe me for that blazer."

He snorted, the corners of his lips twitching upward. "Yeah, yeah. I'll add it to my tab of dealing with your chaos."

And just like that, the moment passed, slipping into something familiar again. But as we walked side by side, a small smile crept onto my lips. Because for the first time, I realized—maybe he wasn't just someone I put up with. Maybe, just maybe, he was someone I could count on.

He groaned. "Unbelievable."

And just like that, everything shifted between us.

After that night, things changed. We still fought, of course. That was inevitable. But underneath it all, there was something different. An unspoken understanding. A quiet kind of care we never acknowledged, but both felt.

"Why do you eat like a gremlin?" he groaned one lunch period, watching me shove fries into my mouth.

"Why do you breathe so loudly?" I shot back.

"Why do you eat like a feral raccoon?" he groaned one lunch period, watching me shove fries into my mouth without a hint of dignity.

"Why do you exist so obnoxiously?" I shot back, wiping my hands on a napkin just to be dramatic.

His eyes narrowed, but there was no real bite behind it. "One of these days, karma's gonna catch up with you."

I smirked, popping another fry into my mouth. "And yet, here I am. Thriving."

He rolled his eyes, but I didn't miss the way his lips twitched—just the smallest hint of a smile.

Emily just shook her head. "I swear, you guys are exhausting."

But the truth was, I had started to appreciate Sam's presence. He was always there—annoying as ever—but in the way a big brother would be. He teased me endlessly, but if someone else tried, he'd shut them down instantly.

One day, he caught me crying after failing a math test. I had my head buried in my arms, trying to muffle the sniffles, when a napkin hit me square in the face.

"Stop crying," he said, flopping down beside me. "You'll make me look bad."

I snatched the napkin off my lap and shot him a glare. "Wow. Thanks for the heartfelt support, idiot."

He rolled his eyes but didn't move away. Instead, he drummed his fingers against the table, staring at the crumpled test paper in front of me. After a moment, he sighed. "Fine. Look, I'll help you study. But if you tell anyone I'm being nice, I'll deny it."

Something in my chest warmed at that. He wasn't saying it to be polite—he meant it. He wasn't going to let me fail.

I wiped my eyes and forced a grin. "Deal."

And just like that, the weight of the bad grade didn't feel so heavy anymore and Sam Carter became the elder brother I never had. The one I never knew I needed.

Years later, at my college graduation, Sam was in the front row, cheering the loudest. As soon as the ceremony ended, I ran up to him, my cap nearly falling off in the process.

He smirked and ruffled my hair. "Not bad, disaster."

I swatted his hand away. "Ugh, do you mind? I just graduated, and you're still treating me like a kid."

He shrugged. "That's because you are. Some things never change."

I rolled my eyes. "Still insufferable."

"And still the only one allowed to hate you," he added with a grin. Then, to my surprise, his expression softened. "I'm proud of you, you know."

My chest tightened at his words. I smirked, trying to lighten the moment. "Wow. A compliment? Do you have a fever?"

Sam chuckled. "Shut up and take the win."

I laughed, shaking my head. "Thanks, Sam. For everything."

He slung an arm around my shoulders and squeezed me into a quick side hug before letting go like it never happened. "Alright, enough of that. Let's go get some food before you get all sentimental and start crying."

"I don't cry!" I protested.

"Yeah, sure," he said, rolling his eyes. "Just like you totally didn't cry when you failed that math test."

I gasped. "That was one time!"

He smirked. "And I'll never let you forget it."

I groaned, but inside, I knew that no matter where life took us, Sam Carter would always be my brother. And I wouldn't have it any other way.

VII

Too Late?

Kabir met Meher when they were twelve. She was a whirlwind from the start—loud, fearless, always two steps ahead of him, always pulling him into something he wasn't quite ready for. She'd grab his hand and drag him into trouble with that mischievous grin, never stopping to think, never hesitating. And somehow, no matter how deep they got, she always found a way out—flashing a sheepish smile, weaving a quick excuse, charming their way past scolding teachers and skeptical parents.

She was his best friend, his constant. When the world felt too big, too uncertain, Meher was the one thing that never wavered. Through scraped knees and stolen mangoes, through whispered secrets at midnight and long walks home in the rain, she was there. Even when he was quiet, overthinking, lost in his own head, she never left him behind.

Meher had this way of making everything feel lighter, like nothing was ever as bad as it seemed. When his parents fought, when he felt like he was never enough, when the weight of growing up pressed too hard on his shoulders, she'd nudge him and say, "Come on, Kabir. The world's not ending yet." And somehow, just hearing her say it made him believe it.

She was chaos and comfort, adventure and home, all at once. And even then, even at twelve, Kabir knew—Meher was different. Meher was forever.

Through high school, through college, through every love that flickered and faded, Meher stayed. She was the constant in a world that kept shifting beneath his feet. She laughed at his terrible taste in girls, shaking her head when he fell too fast, too hard. She rolled her eyes when he swore—every single time—that this one was different. And when it wasn't, when he came back with the same quiet heartbreak in his eyes, she didn't say, "I told you so." Instead, she sat beside him, handed him a cup of chai, and let him fall apart without judgment.

She was the one who saw through his bravado, who understood the spaces between his words. The one who never needed explanations, who never asked him to be anything other than himself. And no matter how many times he got it wrong, no matter how many times he searched for something he couldn't quite name, Meher was always there—steady, unshaken, waiting for him to see what she already knew.

And then, one day, he realized—it had always been her.

But before that realization hit, Meher had just been Meher. His person. His safe place. The one who never judged, never left. He never thought about her as anything more—at least, that's what he told himself.

His boys would always joke about it.

"Bro, you're literally always talking about her."

"Man, just date Meher and get it over with."

"You hold every girl you date to her standard—you ever notice that?"

He'd laugh it off, call them idiots, insist it's not like that.

And yet, somehow, it was like that.

Because when something good happened, she was the first person he wanted to tell—the one who would celebrate with him like his victories were her own. When something bad happened, she never needed explanations; she just knew. She wouldn't fill the silence with empty words or try to fix things that couldn't be fixed. She'd just be there, steady and certain, making the weight a little easier to carry.

Nobody understood his jokes like she did—the way she'd roll her eyes but still laugh, the way she'd fire back with something sharper, funnier, always keeping him on his toes. Nobody challenged him like she did, pushing him to be better, never letting him get away with half-hearted efforts or easy answers.

And through all the fleeting relationships, the almosts and maybes, he liked the girls, he really did. But something was always missing. Some small, unnameable piece that made it feel incomplete, like a song slightly out of tune or a story missing its final page. And no matter how hard he tried to ignore it, that feeling always led him back to the one person who had never felt like almost—Meher.

And still, he didn't get it.

Not when she stole fries off his plate without asking, grinning like she dared him to complain. Not when she danced like an idiot in the middle of the street, arms flailing, just to make him laugh on a day when nothing else could. Not when she showed up at his place at midnight, hair a mess, wearing an old hoodie, because she just knew—knew he was having a rough day, knew he wouldn't ask for company but needed it anyway.

Not even when she looked at him sometimes—really looked at him—like maybe she was waiting. Like maybe she was hoping. Like maybe she was afraid he'd never see it, or worse, that he would and still choose to look away.

But then one day, he did.

And suddenly, every stolen fry, every stupid dance, every midnight visit felt like something more. Like a story he'd been living without realizing he was the main character. Like a truth that had always been there, waiting for him to be brave enough to claim it.

It hit him out of nowhere, like a gut punch. He was on a date with someone—someone pretty, someone kind, someone who, by every reasonable measure, should have been perfect for him. The conversation flowed easily, the candlelight flickered between them, and yet, halfway through dinner, while she was talking about her job, he felt himself drifting.

Not because he wasn't interested. But because his mind was somewhere else.

Because he was thinking about Meher.

Wondering what she was doing at that exact moment. If she was sprawled out on her couch, watching a terrible reality show just to mock it. If she was out with friends, laughing too loudly, stealing fries off someone else's plate the way she always did with his.

Wondering what she would say if she were there, sitting across from him instead—if she'd make a joke about how overthinking was practically his second language. If she'd tease him about his terrible taste in wine. If she'd make the whole night feel easy in a way that nothing ever quite did without her.

And then it hit him. Hard.

Because when he thought about love—not the idea of it, not the expectation of it, but the real thing—she was the person who came to mind.

She had always been the person.

And suddenly, it all made sense.

It had always been her.

The way she laughed—loud, unfiltered, like she never cared who was listening. The way she challenged him, never letting him get away with half-truths or easy answers. The way she made everything—his worst days, his biggest failures, his quietest moments—feel lighter, like the world wasn't such a heavy place after all.

But by the time he finally understood what she meant to him, it wasn't as simple as just telling her.

Because what if she didn't feel the same? What if he saw something in her that she had never seen in him? What if he ruined the one thing in his life that had never let him down, never faltered, never broken?

And even more than that—he wasn't ready.

He wanted to be something first. Someone. Someone she could be proud of, someone she could look at and not just love, but respect.

So he did the only thing he could.

He waited.

Years passed. He built a career, worked on himself, convinced himself that one day, when the moment was perfect, he'd finally tell her.

And then one night, he made up his mind.

No more waiting. No more excuses. No more pretending like he didn't already know the truth.

That night, he paced his apartment, phone in hand, trying to find the right words.

"Hey, I need to tell you something important." No, too serious.

"What if I told you I've been an idiot for years?" Too vague.

"I think I've been in love with you forever, but I was too dumb to see it."

That one felt right.

Kabir took a deep breath, his fingers hovering over his phone screen. His heart pounded against his ribs like it was trying to break free.

This was it. No more waiting. No more excuses.

He typed out the message carefully, pausing before he hit send.

Meet me at our spot. I have something to tell you.

A second later, his phone vibrated in his palm.

On my way.

He let out a shaky breath, running a hand through his hair. His chest felt too tight, his head too full. He grabbed his jacket, his keys, his phone—his hands were trembling.

This was actually happening.

A part of him still couldn't believe he was finally doing this. For years, he'd pushed it down, buried it under fear and hesitation. He had convinced himself that she'd always be there, that there would always be time.

But tonight, he wasn't leaving anything unsaid.

He glanced at himself in the mirror by the door, raking his fingers through his already messy hair. It didn't matter how he looked. Meher wouldn't care. She never did.

Still, the thought of seeing her, of saying the words out loud, made his stomach twist. He imagined it over and over again—the moment he'd finally tell her.

Would she smile? Would she be shocked? Would she roll her eyes and say, Took you long enough, idiot?

Or worse... what if she didn't feel the same?

What if she laughed it off? What if he had spent all these years loving her only to find out she never saw him that way?

He swallowed hard, shaking his head. No. That wasn't Meher. She wouldn't laugh. If she didn't feel the same, she'd be gentle. She'd let him down easy.

But still, the thought terrified him.

His phone buzzed again, pulling him from his spiral. He looked down.

Almost there.

A grin broke across his face.

She was coming.

No more waiting. No more stalling. No more perfect moments. It was time.

He grabbed his keys and stepped toward the door, heart pounding in his chest. His palms were sweaty, his thoughts racing.

This was it.

Tonight, he would tell her. After years of waiting, overthinking, convincing himself he had time—he was finally done with all of it. No more excuses.

He glanced at his phone again, reading her last message for the hundredth time.

Almost there.

That was ten minutes ago.

She should have been here by now.

Kabir bounced his knee anxiously, his fingers tapping against the door handle. Maybe she stopped for gas. Maybe she hit a red light. Maybe she was just messing with him, making him sweat a little.

He checked the time. Another five minutes had passed.

He pulled up their texts again, staring at the blinking cursor. He started typing—Hey, everything okay?—but deleted it. He didn't want to seem paranoid.

Still, a weird feeling crawled up his spine.

He dialed her number.

It rang once. Twice. Then—voicemail.

That was strange. Meher always answered.

He tried again, pacing now, his pulse picking up speed. Voicemail.

A lump formed in his throat. He swallowed it down, telling himself he was overreacting. She was fine. She was probably rolling her eyes at her phone, seeing all his missed calls, laughing to herself about how impatient he was.

But his gut told him something else.

The minutes dragged. His foot tapped anxiously against the floor. His fingers clenched and unclenched.

Another call. Straight to voicemail.

Now his stomach was a knot of unease.

Where the hell was she?

Kabir ran a hand through his hair, forcing himself to take a breath. He'd give it two more minutes. Maybe three. Then he'd go looking for her.

Just as he reached for his keys again—

His phone rang.

His heart lurched. He exhaled in relief, already reaching to answer.

But the name on the screen wasn't Meher's.

It was an unknown number.

He froze.

A strange chill ran down his spine.

For a second, he debated ignoring it. He was too wired, too focused on what he was about to do. But something in his gut twisted—tight, cold, foreboding.

Slowly, with shaking fingers, he swiped to answer.

"Hello?"

Silence. Then, a voice—calm, too calm.

"Is this Kabir Sahni?"

"Uh, yeah, who's this?" he asked, shifting impatiently on his feet.

A pause. Then—

"This is St. Joseph's Hospital. Are you a relative of Meher Gill?"

Kabir's body went cold.

His grip on the phone tightened. "What? No, I—what's going on?"

"There's been an accident."

His ears started ringing. The room tilted.

"No, no, she just—she just texted me," he stammered, his voice breaking. "She's coming to meet me. There's no way—"

"I'm very sorry," the voice said, too calm, too distant. "She was involved in a car crash on Lexington Avenue about ten minutes ago. A drunk driver ran a red light. She—" The voice hesitated. His grip on the phone tightened, his breath catching in his throat. "She didn't make it."

The words didn't make sense.

'She didn't make it.'

His body felt weightless, his mind struggling to process. His entire body went numb. The room around him blurred.

No.

No.

She was almost there.

She was supposed to walk up to him, her hair messy from the wind, her car keys jingling in her hand as she flashed that familiar smirk. She was supposed to walk through the door any second now, teasing him for freaking out. She was supposed to shove him playfully and say, "Alright, what's so important that you dragged me out here this late?"

She was supposed to roll her eyes when he stumbled over his words, then go quiet when she realized what he was trying to say.

She was supposed to be here.

But instead—

The world shattered.

The phone slipped from his grip, crashing to the floor. His knees gave out. He barely registered it. His breathing came in short, shallow gasps, his chest tightening like it was caving in on itself.

This wasn't real. It couldn't be.

His mind raced, searching for another explanation, another possibility. Maybe it was a mistake. Maybe they had the wrong person. Maybe—

'She just texted me.' The words echoed in his head like a cruel joke. Just minutes ago, she had been alive, reading his message, typing back Almost there.

Almost.

But almost didn't count.

The weight of it crashed over him, his body shaking as he struggled to take a breath. His vision blurred. He wanted to call her, to hear her voice, to prove that this was just some sick misunderstanding.

But she wouldn't answer.

Because she was gone.

A sob clawed its way up his throat, but he swallowed it down. His hands curled into fists against the floor, his nails digging into his palms so hard it hurt.

'Why did I wait?'

All those years—telling himself there would be a better time, that he needed to be 'someone' before he told her.

All those nights lying awake, rehearsing how he'd say it.

All those moments where he could have just said it, but didn't.

And now, it didn't matter. Now, she would never know.

His mind flooded with memories—flashes of Meher, vivid and alive, playing in his head like a film reel stuck on repeat.

Her laugh—the one that started as a soft giggle but always turned into something uncontrollable, the kind that made everyone around her laugh too, even if they didn't know why. He could hear it now, ringing in his ears, taunting him with its absence.

Her voice—sarcastic when she teased him, gentle when she knew he needed it, excited when she was talking about something she loved.

"Kabir, you have to listen to this song. It's going to change your life, I swear."

She had said that just a few weeks ago, shoving her phone into his hands, her eyes lighting up with that familiar spark.

"Roz roz" by The Yellow Diary. Just listen to the lyrics, okay? Don't roll your eyes at me."

He had smirked, about to tease her for being dramatic, but then the song started playing, and something in her expression stopped him.

She was watching him carefully, almost nervously, as if waiting for a reaction.

"Roz roz aate ho,
aankhein kyu churate ho
Hai mujhe lage jaise
Khud ko hi chhupate ho

Aisa kya bhala
Mann mein khal raha..."
The words spilled through the speakers, soft but aching.
The same story, day after day. But today, I feel like saying
something new.
She had been humming along under her breath, her
fingers tapping on her knee.
"Kabir," she had said after a while, breaking the silence.
"Some things shouldn't be left unsaid for too long, you
know?"
His chest had tightened. His mind had screamed at him
to say something, to reach for her hand, to tell her that
lately, every love song reminded him of her.
But he hadn't.
He had only laughed, pretending not to understand.
"Damn, Meher. You're getting deep over a song."
She had rolled her eyes, masking whatever had flickered
across her face, but he could hear the disappointment in her
voice when she muttered, "Idiot."
Looking back, he wondered—was she trying to tell him
then? Had she been hoping he'd finally get it, finally say the
words she had been waiting to hear?
The way she looked at him when he said something
stupid—half exasperation and half amusement. You really
are an idiot, aren't you? she'd say, shaking her head, trying
to fight back a grin.
And then there were the other looks. The quieter ones.
The ones that, looking back, felt like maybe they had meant
something all along.
The way she'd watch him when she thought he wasn't
paying attention. The way her eyes softened when he was
rambling about something dumb, like she wasn't listening
to his words but just the sound of his voice. The way she'd

smile at him—not the big, loud, teasing grin she gave the world, but the smaller, softer one. The one that felt just for him.

Had she looked at him, waiting for him to wake up and see what was right in front of him?

His chest ached at the thought. Because maybe—just maybe—if he had seen it sooner, if he had told her sooner, she wouldn't have been in that car at all.

Maybe she would have been here.

Smiling at him.

Laughing at him.

But too late.

Too damn late.

Kabir squeezed his eyes shut, his whole body trembling as the truth settled in like a weight too heavy to bear.

Meher was gone.

And the words he had spent years holding back would never reach her.

Because all the time he thought he had—

Was gone. In a single second.

VIII
Forgiveness

The rain tapped softly against the windowpane, a steady rhythm against the silence of the room. Anaya sat curled up on the couch, arms wrapped around herself, staring at the dimly lit street outside. The city moved on, unaware of the storm raging inside her.

The guilt had settled deep, heavy in her chest, suffocating in its weight. Every stolen glance, every fleeting touch, every moment spent chasing something that was never meant to last—it all came rushing back like a tide she could no longer hold back. The whispered promises that meant nothing. The temporary affections that never filled the emptiness. The meaningless exchanges of passion that left her feeling more hollow than before.

And yet, through it all, there was one constant.

Siddharth.

The man who had never turned away.

She had spent so long convincing herself that love was supposed to be wild, unpredictable, something that set her world on fire. But Siddharth—he was steady, unwavering. He was the quiet presence in the chaos, the safe harbor she had never truly appreciated. He loved her in the kind of way that wasn't loud or demanding, but patient and enduring.

She had tried to hide from it, bury the guilt under distractions, but deep down, she had always known. She had feared this moment, feared that one day he would look at her and see everything she had been trying to keep from him.

And now, as the rain blurred the world outside, she realized it was time to stop running.

Because no matter how far she had strayed, every road, every mistake, every lost moment—had always led her back to him.

Anaya turned to look at him. He was in the kitchen, moving with quiet certainty, making tea the way he always did when she sat in silence for too long. The soft clink of porcelain, the low simmer of water—sounds that had filled their home for years, sounds she had barely noticed until now.

His back was strong, steady. A presence that had never wavered, never faltered, even when she had.

How long had she taken that for granted?

Her fingers curled into the fabric of her sweater, gripping tightly as if to ground herself. The words sat heavy on her tongue, but the weight of silence was worse.

"Siddharth..." she began, barely above a whisper.

He paused, mid-motion, then continued pouring the tea. "What is it?" His voice was gentle, familiar—an invitation, not a demand.

She wanted to believe that kindness would still be there once she spoke. That the warmth in his tone wouldn't turn cold.

Her throat felt tight. Dry. She forced herself to swallow, but it did nothing to ease the ache inside her.

"I—" The words trembled at the edge of her lips, her breath shuddering. "I've done things. Terrible things."

The admission felt raw, like peeling back skin to expose the wound beneath.

Siddharth didn't speak right away. He set the kettle down with practiced ease, as if giving her space to continue. But she could see the way his shoulders tensed, the slightest hesitation in his movements.

She pressed on, even as shame twisted inside her. "I don't even know where to start."

Siddharth finally turned to face her, his expression unreadable. Not angry, not yet—but something flickered in his eyes. Something that made her stomach drop.

For years, she had feared this moment. Now, there was no turning back.

Siddharth didn't move, but his stillness carried a weight that pressed down on the space between them. Without a word, he turned off the kettle, poured the tea, and carried the cups to the table. The small, familiar ritual felt almost cruel now, like muscle memory refusing to acknowledge the moment unraveling around them.

He sat across from her, hands resting on the table, steady as ever. "Then start anywhere," he said, his voice calm—but not untouched.

Anaya's fingers twisted together in her lap, her knuckles white. She couldn't meet his eyes. Couldn't bear to see whatever might be written in them.

"I don't know why I do the things I do," she said, her voice barely holding together. "Or maybe I do, and I just don't want to face it." She let out a bitter, shaky laugh. "I've spent so much time running—from guilt, from regret, from myself—that I don't even know who I am anymore."

Her breath shuddered, her chest tightening with the weight of everything she had never said. "I've been unfaithful, Siddharth." The words broke something open inside her, but the pain had been there all along, waiting. "I kept searching for happiness in places it was never meant to be. Like if I could just find the right person, if I could feel something strong enough, it would fix me. Make me whole."

She swallowed hard, her throat burning. "But every time, it just left me emptier. More lost. More... ashamed."

Silence settled between them, heavy and unyielding.

For the first time, she forced herself to look at him. To see what was left.

Tears blurred her vision as she finally forced herself to meet his eyes. "And the worst part?" Her voice wavered, raw and unsteady. "You were here. Through everything. The one person who never turned away. And I still—" She sucked in a sharp breath, her chest tightening. "I still kept searching for something else. Something I couldn't even name. And now..." Her voice broke, the weight of it all crashing over her. "Now, all I feel is shame. I hate myself, Siddharth. I hate the person I've become."

Her shoulders trembled as she let the confession settle between them, her breath ragged, uneven. She wanted him to say something. Anything.

But Siddharth remained still, his expression unreadable.

The silence was unbearable. She wished he would yell, break something, demand to know why she had done this. She wished he would accuse her, tell her exactly how much she had hurt him. Anger, pain—anything would be easier than this quiet, this impossible, suffocating stillness.

"Say something," she whispered, her hands gripping the edge of the table. "Please. I need you to say something. I don't deserve your kindness—I know I don't—but I need to know what you're thinking."

The rain continued to patter against the window, the only sound filling the tense space between them. Anaya braced herself for his response, terrified of what he might say but even more afraid of what he wouldn't.

And then, finally, he spoke. "Why?"

She blinked. "What?"

"Why did you do it?" His voice wasn't angry, just... steady. Patient. "You said you were searching for something. What was it?"

She let out a bitter laugh, wiping at her tears. "I don't know. I thought it was happiness. Or excitement. Or... something. I convinced myself that I had never really been happy before I got married, so how could I be happy now? Maybe I thought if someone else wanted me, if I had their attention, it would mean I was worth something. But it was all just an illusion. None of them cared about me. Not really. They didn't know me. And I didn't know them."

She inhaled shakily. "But you... You were always there. You were always real. And I never stopped to see it."

Siddharth studied her for a long moment, his expression unreadable. She could feel her heartbeat pounding in her ears. Then, at last, he nodded, as if he had been waiting for this moment all along.

Anaya clenched her fists. "I don't know if I can ever make this right, Siddharth. I don't even know if I should ask for your forgiveness. But I had to tell you. I couldn't keep living like this. I couldn't keep pretending."

Her breath came fast, her chest rising and falling as she waited for his reaction. But still, he said nothing. Just sat there, his gaze holding hers like an anchor in the storm of her emotions.

She squeezed her eyes shut. "Please say something. Yell at me. Get angry. Hate me. I deserve it."

There was a long pause. Then, finally, Siddharth exhaled and said, "I know."

Her eyes snapped open, shock flooding through her veins. "What?"

Siddharth's voice remained calm, steady. "I know, Anaya. I've known for a long time."

And just like that, the weight of her confession wasn't the heaviest thing in the room anymore. It was the realization that he had always known—and still, he had stayed.

Siddharth studied her for a long moment, his expression unreadable yet impossibly tender. Then, with a quiet sigh, he reached across the table, his fingers brushing lightly over hers. It was the simplest of touches, yet it shattered something inside her.

He walked over, placing the cup in front of her before sitting across the table. His eyes, warm and gentle, met hers. "I know, Anaya. I've known for a long time." She felt exposed, raw. "Then why didn't you say anything? Why didn't you leave? Why didn't you hate me?"

Anaya's lip quivered. "But I don't deserve that kind of love. I don't deserve you."

"You think love is about deserving," he said softly. "But it's never been about that for me. Love isn't something you earn, Anaya. It's something you give. Freely. Without conditions."

Siddharth shook his head. "Love isn't about deserving, Anaya. It's about choosing. And I chose you. Even when it hurt. Even when I knew what was happening. I chose you every single day, and I kept hoping that one day, you'd choose me too."

Her breath hitched as fresh tears slipped down her cheeks. "But I broke us," she whispered. "I broke *you*."

His fingers curled gently around hers. "You didn't break me," he said, his voice steady. "You were hurting. Lost. And I saw that, even when you couldn't. Even when you didn't want me to."

Anaya shook her head, guilt clawing at her insides. "I don't know how to fix this."

Siddharth's thumb traced slow, soothing circles over her knuckles. "Then let's start with this moment," he murmured. "Right here. Right now. No running. No hiding. Just us."

She let out a shaky breath, staring at their joined hands. The warmth of his touch, the unwavering steadiness of him—it was the first time in a long while that she felt something close to safe.

And for the first time, she wanted to stay.

The sincerity in his words broke something inside her. A sob choked its way up her throat, and before she knew it, she was crying—truly crying—in front of him for the first time. Not out of frustration or loneliness, but out of something else. Something deeper. Something she had never truly felt before.

Love. Real love.

Her body trembled as she covered her face with her hands, overwhelmed. "Siddharth, I'm so sorry. I don't know how to fix this. I don't even know where to start."

Siddharth reached across the table, taking her shaking hands in his. "Start by letting me take care of you, completely. Let me love you the way I always have."

Anaya let out a strangled sob and nodded, collapsing into his embrace. For the first time in her life, she allowed herself to be held, to be loved, without fear of what would happen next.

She wasn't running anymore.

She was home.

Anaya's life had always been a series of fleeting connections. She had never truly known what it meant to be loved or to love in return. She had grown up believing love was something you chased—something thrilling and temporary, something that burned bright and then vanished like embers in the wind.

Every relationship before Siddharth had ended the same way—her running.

She had been running for as long as she could remember, running from relationships that began to feel too heavy, too real, too suffocating. The moment someone started to care, the moment she sensed permanence, she left. She had convinced herself that love was not meant to last, that once the passion dulled and the excitement faded, there was no point in staying.

But then came Siddharth.

Siddharth, who was quiet, steady, patient.

Siddharth, who never demanded, never begged. He simply gave.

At first, that confused her. She had expected him to be like all the others—distant when she became difficult, angry when she pushed him away. But he wasn't. No matter how hard she tested him, he never walked away. No matter how much she withdrew, he remained.

And now, she understood why.

Anaya's breath trembled as she forced herself to meet his gaze, expecting to find disappointment, hurt—maybe even contempt. But all she saw was him. Steady, unshaken, the same man who had loved her through every storm, every moment she had pushed him away.

"You keep saying you don't deserve me," Siddharth murmured, his thumb grazing her damp cheek. "But love isn't about *deserving*, Anaya. It's not a prize you win or a punishment you escape. It's a choice."

Her lips quivered as fresh tears slipped down her face. "And I kept choosing wrong."

His hand lingered, gentle yet firm. "Maybe," he said. "But you're here now. And that means something."

She let out a broken laugh, shaking her head. "I don't even know *who* I am anymore, Siddharth."

He studied her for a moment before speaking, his voice soft but certain. "Then let's figure it out together."

Something inside her cracked wide open at those words. No grand declarations. No conditions. Just a quiet promise—one she wasn't sure she had earned, but one she wanted to believe in.

"You deserve love, Anaya," he said softly. "The kind that stays. The kind that forgives. And if you'll have me, I want to be the one who proves it to you."

She searched his face, desperate to find a reason to believe he was lying, that he was just waiting for her to break so he could finally throw her mistakes back at her. But all she saw was love.

Pure, unselfish, unwavering love.

Tears streamed down her face as her body trembled with the weight of the realization. She had spent her entire life believing love was meant to be chased, to be grasped at desperately before it slipped away. But Siddharth had never made her chase him.

He had waited.

And she had never, in all her years of running, felt so still.

A shaky breath left her lips. "Yes," she whispered. "Yes."

She collapsed into his embrace, her sobs muffled against his chest as he held her, his touch as gentle as ever. For the first time in her life, she wasn't holding on out of desperation or fear. She was letting go.

Letting go of the need to chase something fleeting.

Letting go of the fear that love was meant to end.

Letting go of the belief that she was incapable of being loved.

It was not an easy journey.

Anaya had to unlearn everything she thought she knew about love and intimacy. There were days when she still flinched at the idea of permanence, when the weight of her past choices felt unbearable, but Siddharth never faltered.

He was there, holding her hand, reminding her that love wasn't about perfection—it was about choosing each other, day after day.

And slowly, she learned.

She learned to stop looking for validation in the eyes of strangers.

She learned to stop searching for the high of infatuation when real joy had been waiting for her all along.

She learned to love Siddharth the way he had always loved her.

One evening, as they lay in bed, Anaya turned to him, her fingers tracing lazy circles against his palm.

"Do you ever regret waiting for me?" she asked softly.

Siddharth looked at her with a smile so gentle it made her chest ache. "Never," he said.

She let out a shaky laugh, pressing a kiss to his knuckles. "I must have been unbearable."

"You were lost," he corrected, brushing a strand of hair behind her ear. "And I knew you'd find your way back."

She swallowed past the lump in her throat. "You never doubted me?"

"Not even once."

Her eyes burned with unshed tears, but this time, they weren't from guilt or regret. They were from something new. Something she had only begun to understand.

She wasn't running anymore. She was home.

Years passed, and Siddharth continued to take care of her, just as he always had. And for the first time in her life, Anaya let him. She let herself be loved without suspicion or guilt. She let herself believe that love could be kind, that it didn't have to hurt, that it didn't have to be earned through suffering.

She no longer saw the past as a series of mistakes but as a path—one that had led her home.

To him.

To a love that had never wavered, never faltered, even when she had.

And for the first time in her life, she wasn't running. She wasn't searching.

She was exactly where she was meant to be.